CHANTS for Grammar

Mikiko Nakamoto

CONTENTS

Warm Up!	FIGHT! FIGHT!	CD 2	2
Chant 1	ABCDEFG...	CD 3/4/5	4
Chant 2	My name **is** Larry.	CD 6/7/8	6
Chant 3	**What** is this?	CD 9/10/11	8
Chant 4	I **have** a pet.	CD 12/13/14	10
Song 5	This is **my** friend.	CD 15/16/17	12
Chant 6	Look! More than one.	CD 18/19/20	14
Chant 7	What're **these**?	CD 21/22/23	16
Chant 8	The **little** one? The **big** one?	CD 24/25/26	18
Chant 9	**What do you have** in your bag?	CD 27/28/29	20
Chant 10	I **am walking**.	CD 30/31/32	22
Chant 11	You **can** do it.	CD 33/34/35	24
Songs 12	Vocabulary songs	CD 36/37/38	26
Chant 13	**Don't** do that.	CD 39/40/41	28
Chant 14	He **has**, She **has**...	CD 42/43/44	30
Chant 15	**Does** he like me?	CD 45/46/47	32
Chant 16	Where? When? How?	CD 48/49/50	34
Chant 17	**Who** has a birthday in May?	CD 51/52/53	36
Chant 18	**What** a pretty girl!	CD 54/55/56	38
Chant 19	Mom **was cooking** all day long.	CD 57/58/59	40
Chant 20	I **went** to the market.	CD 60/61/62	42
Chant 21	**Did you** make your bed?	CD 63/64/65	44
Chant 22	I **will** go outside.	CD 66/67/68	46
Chant 23	This is my bike. It's **mine**.	CD 69/70/71	48
Chant 24	This one is **bigger than** the other one.	CD 72/73/74	50
Chant 25	My dog is **as** big **as** yours.	CD 75/76	52
Chant 26	We go to the bakery **to buy some bread**.	CD 77/78/79	54
Chant 27	I want something **to eat**.	CD 80/81/82	56
Chant 28	I don't know **what to do**.	CD 83/84/85	58
Chant 29	I want you **to study hard**.	CD 86/87/88	60
Chant 30	The wine **is made** from grapes.	CD 89/90	62
Chant 31	This is the boy **whom** I love.	CD 91/92	64
Chant 32	**Have you ever seen** a snake?	CD 93/94/95	66
Chant 33	That makes him happy.	CD 96/97	68
Chant 34	Let's go out **if** it is clear.	CD 98/99	70

APRICOT

Warm Up!

F

I

G

H

T

Give me an **F**.

Give me an **I**.

CD 2

Give me a **G**.

Give me an **H**.

Give me a **T**.

What have you got?

F I G H T

FIGHT

FIGHT!

FIGHT!

FIGHT!

FIGHT! FIGHT!

アルファベットには全部で26文字あり、それぞれに ●**Upper-case letter**（大文字）と

① Fill in the blanks.

A B   D   G H

K   N   Q

S T   Z

● **Lower-case letter**（小文字）があります。

2 Fill in the blanks.

a   c   e   f   h

j   m   o   r

u   v   y

A B C D E F G H I J K L M N
O P Q R S T U V W X Y Z

yellow   blue   red   green   yellow   blue   red

yellow   blue   green   yellow   blue   red

red

yellow   green   yellow   blue   red

blue   red

yellow   blue   red   blue

green

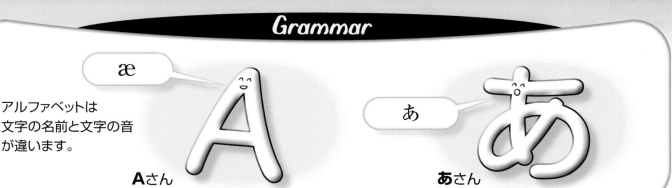

Grammar

æ **A** Aさん

あ **あ** あさん

アルファベットは
文字の名前と文字の音
が違います。

❶ 次の ◯ にアルファベットを1字書いて単語を完成しましょう。（小文字）━CD━5

❶ _____ ook

❷ _____ and

❸ _____ pple

❹ _____ at

❺ _____ oor

❻ _____ gg

❼ _____ mbrella

❽ _____ lass

❾ _____ onkey

❿ _____ nk

⓫ _____ iger

⓬ _____ ing

⓭ _____ emon

⓮ _____ izza

⓯ _____ atch

⓰ _____ nion

⓱ _____ am

⓲ _____ ebra

⓳ _____ acht

⓴ _____ un

㉑ _____ otebook

㉒ _____ ing

㉓ _____ iolin

㉔ _____ inger

㉕ _____ fo

㉖ _____ ueen

My name is Larry. Be動詞

CD 6

Hi. My name is Larry.
What's your name?

My name is Lisa.
Nice to meet you.

Nice to meet you, too.

Chant
CD 7/8

My name is Larry. What's your name?

My name is Lisa. What's your name?

My name is Judie. What's your name?

My name is Takeshi. What's your name?

I am Larry. You are Lisa.

I am Lisa. You are Judie.

I am Judie. You are Takeshi.

I am Takeshi. You are Larry.

（What is ＝ What's）

six

6

Grammar

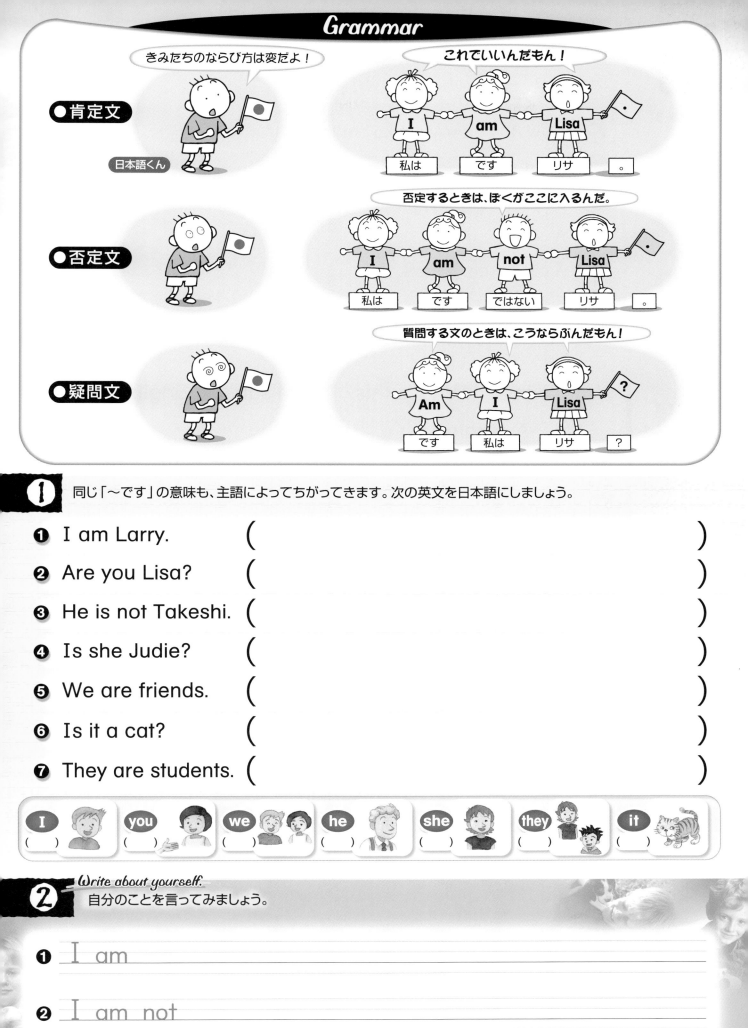

① 同じ「〜です」の意味も、主語によってちがってきます。次の英文を日本語にしましょう。

❶ I am Larry.　　　　　　（　　　　　　　　　　　　　　　　　　　　）

❷ Are you Lisa?　　　　　（　　　　　　　　　　　　　　　　　　　　）

❸ He is not Takeshi.　　 （　　　　　　　　　　　　　　　　　　　　）

❹ Is she Judie?　　　　　（　　　　　　　　　　　　　　　　　　　　）

❺ We are friends.　　　　（　　　　　　　　　　　　　　　　　　　　）

❻ Is it a cat?　　　　　　（　　　　　　　　　　　　　　　　　　　　）

❼ They are students.　　（　　　　　　　　　　　　　　　　　　　　）

I	you	we	he	she	they	it
(　)	(　)	(　)	(　)	(　)	(　)	

Write about yourself.
② 自分のことを言ってみましょう。

❶ I am

❷ I am not

7　seven

How do you say "neko" in English?

A cat.

Once more please.

A cat.

A cat. I see. Thank you.

Chant
CD 10/11

What's this?   What's this? What's this in English?

A stapler.

Once more please.

A stapler.

Louder please.

A stapler.   A stapler!   A STAPLER!

Grammar

英語で「何」はなに？

What?

❶ 絵を見て答えを書きましょう。

❶ 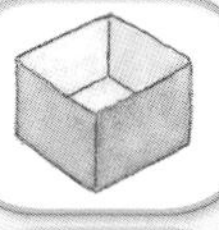 What is this?　　It is

❷

❸

❹

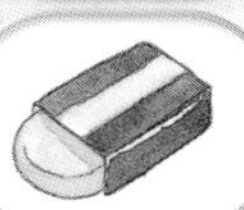

❺

❻

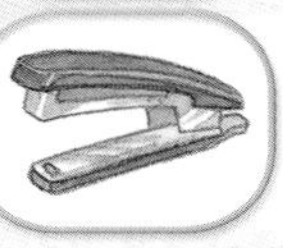

| a box | a ruler | an eraser | a desk | a chair | a stapler |

この **，** は、ここに何かが省略されているしるしです。

What is ➡ What's
It is ➡ It's

a book

ものの名前の前には「1つですよ」のしるしに **a** を書きます。

an eraser

母音（「あ い う え お」の音）のどれかから始まる時は **a** ではなく **an** になります。

❷ 先生に次のように聞いてみましょう。

❶ How do you say "　　　　　　　　　　　" in English?

❷

4 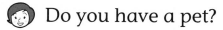 一般動詞

CD-12

Do you have a pet?

No, I don't.

Do you want a pet?

Yes, I do. I want a rabbit.

I have a pet.

A big black cat.

It's big. ××   It's black. ××

I have a pet.

A big black cat.

You have a pet.

A long green snake.

It's long. ××   It's green. ××

You have a pet.

A long green snake.

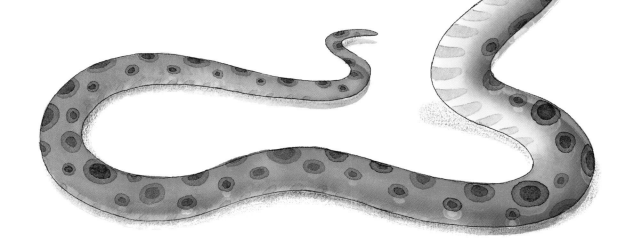

Grammar

don't が入ると「～ではない」という意味になります。

ねえ、入れてー！

だめ！「～ではない」っていう意味になってしまうから。

I don't like cats.

私は　　～ではない　　～を好きです　　ねこ

(don't = do not)

---

① 次の文に like あるいは don't like を入れて、文を完成しましょう。

❶ I _____ carrots.

❷ I _____ pizza.

❸ I _____ games.

---

② *Write about yourself.*
自分にあてはまる方を○で囲みましょう。

❶ I (don't play / play) soccer.

❷ I (don't cook / cook) dinner by myself.

❸ I (don't go to / go to) school by train.

❹ Do you have a pet?　（Yes, I do. / No, I don't. ）

❺ Do you want a pet?　（Yes, I do. / No, I don't. ）

❻ Do you play basketball?　（Yes, I do. / No, I don't. ）

---

③ *Write about yourself.*
あなたがほしいものを1つ、ほしくないものを1つ書きましょう。

ほしいもの　What do you want?

_____

_____

ほしくないもの　What don't you want?

_____

_____

CD 15

Judie, this is my friend.
Her name is Lisa. She is from Japan.

Hi, Lisa. My name is Judie. Nice to meet you.

My name is Lisa. Nice to meet you, too.

Song

CD 16/17

This is my friend. His name is Larry.

Larry, Larry, Larry.

Our friend's name is Larry.

This is my friend. Her name is Lisa.

Lisa, Lisa, Lisa.

Our friend's name is Lisa.

Grammar

ぼくは は ぼくの に

変わらなきゃ いけないんだ。

I   my

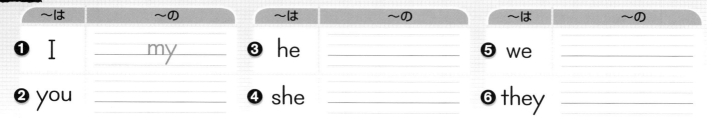

「～は」と「～の」の悲劇
- you は **your** に変わるんだ。
- he は **his** 、she は **her** になります。
- we は **our** 、they は **their** になります。
- 人の名前（Tom）は **Tom's** になります。

① 空欄をうめましょう。

～は	～の		～は	～の		～は	～の
❶ I	my		❸ he			❺ we	
❷ you			❹ she			❻ they	

② 次の ＿＿ に、（ ）内の日本語を英語にして書きましょう。

❶ This is ＿＿＿＿ dog. (私の)　❷ This isn't ＿＿＿＿ notebook. (彼女の)

❸ Is this ＿＿＿＿ computer? (彼の)　❹ That's ＿＿＿＿ bag. (あなたの)

❺ These are ＿＿＿＿ ＿＿＿＿ CDs. (私の兄の)

❻ Is that ＿＿＿＿ book? (トムの)　❼ That's ＿＿＿＿ classroom. (私たちの)

③ （ ）の中から適する語を選びましょう。

❶ Whose hat is this?　　It is (he / his) hat.

❷ Whose book is this?　　It is (she / her) book.

❸ Whose bicycles are these?　　They are (we / our) bicycles. *

④ *Write about yourself.*
あなたのお友達を紹介する文を書きましょう。

This is my friend.　　Her name is Lisa.

お友達の顔をかきましょう。

6 Look! More than one. 名詞の複数形

CD 18

Is that your dog?

Yes. That one is my dog, too.

How many dogs do you have?

I have six dogs.

Chant
CD 19/20

A dog?	Look!	More than one.	DOGS!
A cat?	Look!	More than one.	CATS!
A pig?	Look!	More than one.	PIGS!
A goose?	Look!	More than one.	GEESE!
A mouse?	Look!	More than one.	MICE!!
A sheep?	Look!	More than one.	Well… SHEEP!

Grammar

へんな **s** がくっついてる！

an　apple　apple　apple　s

ヘッ！
ぼくたちはずっと同じだもん。

sheep
sheep

▌1つのものをあらわすときは、**a** か **an** が前に入ってきますが、
2つ以上のものには、単語のうしろに **s** がくっつきます。

---

① 次の複数の形を書きましょう。

❶ book → (　　　　　　　　　　)

❷ table → (　　　　　　　　　　)

❸ cup → (　　　　　　　　　　)

❹ chair → (　　　　　　　　　　)

❺ friend → (　　　　　　　　　　)

❻ sister → (　　　　　　　　　　)

❼ class → (　　　　　　　　　　)

❽ watch → (　　　　　　　　　　)

❾ knife → (　　　　　　　　　　)

❿ mouse → (　　　　　　　　　　)

⓫ fish → (　　　　　　　　　　)

② (　)の中から適する語を選びましょう。

❶ I have ten (pencil / pencils).

❷ I see many (star / stars).

❸ I want some (stamp / stamps).

❹ Do you have any (book / books)?

❺ I have (a / an) egg.

❻ I see a (men / man).

❼ How many (mice / mouse) do you see?

❽ I have two big (box / boxes / boxs).

❾ You have six (dictionary / dictionaries).

I	\/	/\	\/	\/ /	\/ /
one	two	three	four	five	six
\/\/	\/ /	\/\/	\/\/
seven	eight	nine	ten

③ Write about yourself.
あなたのことを書きましょう。

❶ How many sisters do you have?

I have

❷ How many brothers do you have?

❸ How many (　　　　　　　) do you have?

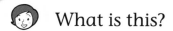

What is this?

It is my English textbook.

Are those your textbooks, too?

Yes, they are my textbooks.

Chant

CD 22/23

What's this? What's this? What is this?
It's a book. It's a book.
It's my book.

What's that? What's that? What is that?
It's a pencil. It's a pencil.
It's my pencil.

What're these? What're these? What are these?
They are markers. They are markers.
They are my markers.   (What're = What are)

What're those? What're those? What are those?
They are rulers. They are rulers.
They are my rulers.

「待って〜!」

That is ….	Those are ….
「あれは … です」	「あれらは … です」
This is ….	These are ….
「これは … です」	「これらは … です」

1

絵を見て、次の文を完成しましょう。

❶ This is an ant.

These are _____

❷ This is a car.

_____

❸ That is a star.

_____

❹ That is a tree.

_____

❺ What is this? It is a ball.

What are these? They are _____

❻  What is that? _____

What are those? _____

2

Write about yourself.

あなたの好きなことばを入れて文と絵をかきましょう。

What is this?

It is my _____

What are those?

They are my _____

The little one? The big one?

形容詞 ①

Which dog is yours?

The big brown one is mine. *

Is he noisy?

No. He is a quiet dog.

Chant
CD 25/26

Which dog is yours?

The little one? The big one?
The ugly one or the pretty one?

The noisy one? The quiet one?
The gentle one or the scary one?

The dirty one? The clean one?
The fat one or the skinny one?

The long one? The short one?
The heavy one or the light one?

❶ 左のページからあてはまる英語を見つけて書きましょう。

❶ みにくい ＿＿＿＿＿＿＿＿＿　❷ 小さい ＿＿＿＿＿＿＿＿＿　❸ みじかい ＿＿＿＿＿＿＿＿＿

❹ 大きい ＿＿＿＿＿＿＿＿＿　❺ きたない ＿＿＿＿＿＿＿＿＿　❻ 重い ＿＿＿＿＿＿＿＿＿

❼ うるさい ＿＿＿＿＿＿＿＿＿　❽ しずかな ＿＿＿＿＿＿＿＿＿　❾ かるい ＿＿＿＿＿＿＿＿＿

❿ やさしい ＿＿＿＿＿＿＿＿＿　⓫ こわい ＿＿＿＿＿＿＿＿＿　⓬ やせた ＿＿＿＿＿＿＿＿＿

⓭ 長い ＿＿＿＿＿＿＿＿＿　⓮ せいけつな ＿＿＿＿＿＿＿＿＿　⓯ ふとい ＿＿＿＿＿＿＿＿＿

❷ （　）内の語が入る位置を記号で書きましょう。

❶ I ㋐ have ㋑ a ㋒ ball ㋓ .　　　（ pretty ）　□

❷ I ㋐ read ㋑ an ㋒ book ㋓ .　　（ interesting ）　□

❸ That ㋐ is ㋑ my ㋒ watch ㋓ .　　（ new ）　□

❸ *Write about yourself.*
「これは〜です」で、自分が紹介したいものを英語で書いてみましょう。

❶
This is my ＿＿＿＿＿＿＿＿＿＿＿＿＿＿＿＿＿＿＿＿＿
It is ＿＿＿＿＿＿＿＿＿＿＿＿＿＿＿＿＿＿＿＿＿＿＿

❷
This is ＿＿＿＿＿＿＿＿＿＿＿＿＿＿＿＿＿＿＿＿＿＿＿
It is ＿＿＿＿＿＿＿＿＿＿＿＿＿＿＿＿＿＿＿＿＿＿＿＿

❹ あなた自身のことを考えて書いてみましょう。

❶ I am ＿＿＿＿＿＿＿＿＿＿＿＿＿＿＿＿＿＿＿＿＿＿＿＿＿＿＿

❷ I am ＿＿＿＿＿＿＿＿＿＿＿＿＿＿＿＿＿＿＿＿＿＿＿＿＿＿＿

❸ I am not ＿＿＿＿＿＿＿＿＿＿＿＿＿＿＿＿＿＿＿＿＿＿＿＿＿

CD 27

What do you have in your hand?

Guess what? A little creature.

A frog !!

Chant
CD 28/29

What do you have in your bag? ××
What do you have in your bag? ×
What do you have in your bag? ××
Show me what you have. *

Textbooks, notebooks, pencils, and an eraser.
A ruler, a dictionary, an atlas and a lunch box.
No games, no comics, no snacks, SEE?

ATLAS

Grammar

わからない時は質問の形でぼくの後についてきてくださぁーい！

① 次の（＝）に（ ）内の意味を表す英語を書き入れましょう。

❶ I don't （＿＿＿＿＿＿＿） math. （好き）

❷ Do you （＿＿＿＿＿＿＿） my teacher? （知っている）

❸ Where do you （＿＿＿＿＿＿＿）? （住んでいる）

❹ I （＿＿＿＿＿＿＿） soccer after school. （する）

❺ I （＿＿＿＿＿＿＿） to school. （歩く）

② What を使って次の文を疑問文にしましょう。

❶ You have a camera in your bag.

_____

❷ You need a dictionary .

_____

❸ You want a Japanese stamp .

_____

❹ You play baseball after school.

_____

Write about yourself.

③ What do you have in your bag?

I have _____

_____

_____ in my bag.

CD 30

 What are you doing?

 I am doing my homework.

Chant
CD 31/32

I am walking.

You are walking.

He is walking.

She is walking.

They are walking. ××

We are walking on the earth. ××××

Look! It is walking, too!

I am singing.

You are singing.

He is singing.

She is singing.

They are singing. ××

We are singing on the earth. ××××

Look! It is singing, too!

Grammar

walk ing

「今～している」ところを表すのは

$\left\{\begin{array}{c} \text{is} \\ \text{am} \\ \text{are} \end{array}\right\}$ ＋ 動詞 ＋ ing のかたちです。

ぼくたちも大切なんだからね。

動詞に ing がくっつくと「～している」という意味です。

---

① ＝＝＝ に適する語を書いて「～している」の意味にしましょう。

I cook breakfast.

❶ I ＿＿＿＿＿＿ ＿＿＿＿＿＿ breakfast.

Larry and I go to the city hall.

❷ Larry and I ＿＿＿＿＿＿ ＿＿＿＿＿＿ to the city hall.

I don't play the piano.

❸ I ＿＿＿＿＿＿ ＿＿＿＿＿＿ ＿＿＿＿＿＿ the piano.

The boys sleep under a tall tree.

❹ The boys ＿＿＿＿＿＿ ＿＿＿＿＿＿ under a tall tree.

---

② ☐ の中の語を使って、次の質問に答えましょう。

read
sing
sleep
cry
run

❶ What is the bear doing? ＿＿＿＿＿＿＿＿＿＿

❷ What is the duck doing? ＿＿＿＿＿＿＿＿＿＿

❸ What are the mice doing? ＿＿＿＿＿＿＿＿＿＿

❹ What is the boy doing? ＿＿＿＿＿＿＿＿＿＿

❺ What are you doing now? ＿＿＿＿＿＿＿＿＿＿

11 You can do it. 助動詞 can

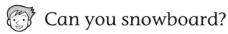

CD 33

Can you snowboard?

No, I can't. Can you?

Of course I can. I can ski, too.

Chant
CD 34/35

I can't swim.

    Yes, you can.

I can't swim.

    Yes, you can.

I can't swim.

    Yes, you can.

    Try it. Try it. You can do it.

I made it, I made it, I made it. All right!

    You made it, you made it, you made it. All right.

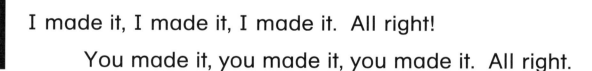

Grammar

ちょっと入れて！

「できる」と言いたいときは、ぼくがいる〜！

I can go

can

できる もんねー！

cannot

できないー …

(cannot = can't)

1　次の文に can あるいは can't を入れて、文を完成しましょう。

❶ I _____ play the piano.

❷ A hippo _____ fly in the sky.

❸ A frog _____ swim in a lake.

❹ A dog _____ climb trees.

2　次の語をならべかえて正しい文を作りましょう。

❶ this / use / Can / computer / you
_____ ?

❷ mother / well / My / swim / cannot
_____ .

❸ can / cook / What / you
_____ ?

❹ English / Can / father / your / speak
_____ ?

3　*Write about yourself.*
あなたができることを3つ書きましょう。

❶ _____

❷ _____

❸ _____

Song 1
CD 36

Days of the Week

Sunday   Monday   Tuesday   Wednesday

Thursday   Friday   Saturday

Song 2
CD 37

The Weather Song

Sunny days, rainy days, windy days and snowy days.

A hot day, and a cold day, beautiful days for you and me.

Song 3
CD 38

The Twelve Months of the Year

January   February   March   April   May   June   July

August   September   October   November and December

❶ 12か月の説明が正しくなるように考えて、英文を完成しましょう。

❶ _____ is the first month. ❷ _____ is the sixth month.

❸ _____ is the seventh month. ❹ _____ is the second month.

❺ _____ is the ninth month. ❻ _____ is the fourth month.

❼ _____ is the eighth month. ❽ _____ is the last month.

January   February   March   April   May   June   July   August   September   October   November   December

❷ 曜日を日曜日から順に並べて書きましょう。

_____ ➡ _____ ➡ _____

➡ _____ ➡ _____ ➡ _____

➡ _____

Friday   Sunday   Thursday   Monday   Wednesday   Tuesday   Saturday

❸ 天候を表す英語を右下から選んで書きましょう。

❶ _____   ❷ _____   ❸ _____   ❹ _____

❺ _____   ❻ _____   ❼ _____

cloudy
cold   rainy
hot
windy   sunny
snowy

❹ 今日のことについて次の質問に答えましょう。

❶ What is the date today?   It is _____

❷ What day is it today?   It is _____

❸ How is the weather today?   It is _____

Tell me everything. Be honest.

OK. But don't tell anybody. It's a secret.
Well, I had a date yesterday. *

What? You had a date?

Don't speak so loudly. Be quiet.

Chant

CD 40/41

Do this. Do that. Don't do that.
Do this. Do that. Don't do that.

Mom is always yelling at me.

Do your homework.   Don't go out.

Make your bed.   Don't jump around.

Eat more slowly.   Don't make noise.

Go to bed.   Don't stay up late.

Behave yourself.   Be a good boy.

Do this. Do that. Don't do that.
Do this. Do that. Don't do that.

Can't you hear her yelling at me?

Grammar

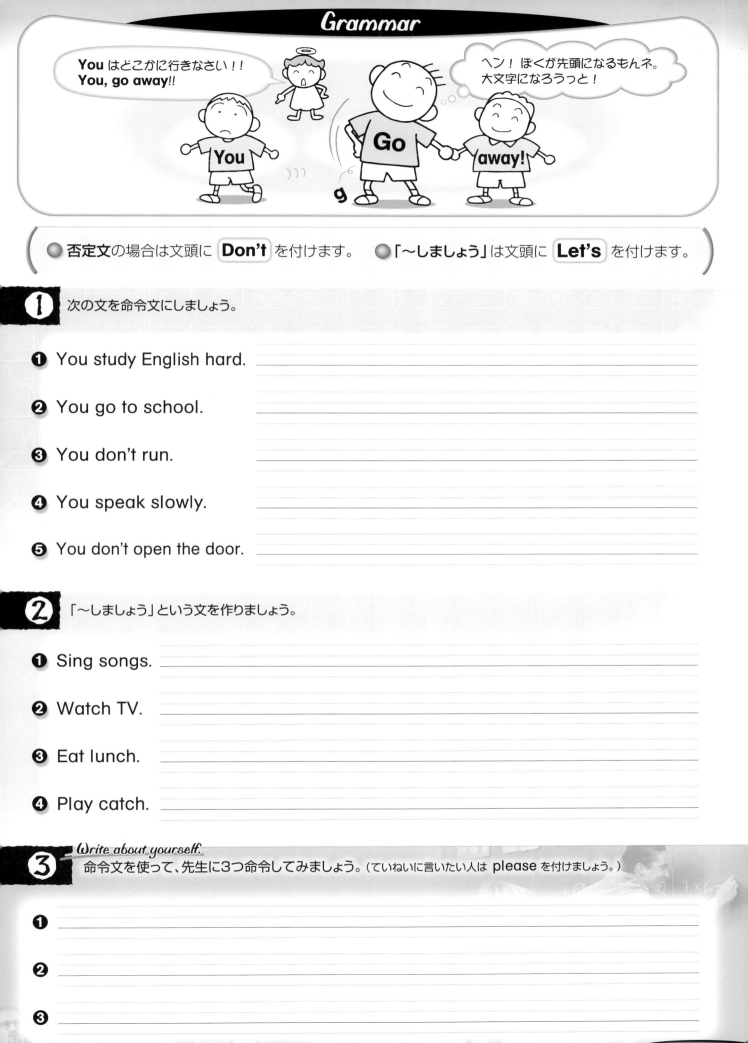

- 否定文の場合は文頭に **Don't** を付けます。　●「〜しましょう」は文頭に **Let's** を付けます。

1 次の文を命令文にしましょう。

❶ You study English hard. ＿＿＿＿＿＿＿＿＿＿＿＿＿＿＿＿＿

❷ You go to school. ＿＿＿＿＿＿＿＿＿＿＿＿＿＿＿＿＿

❸ You don't run. ＿＿＿＿＿＿＿＿＿＿＿＿＿＿＿＿＿

❹ You speak slowly. ＿＿＿＿＿＿＿＿＿＿＿＿＿＿＿＿＿

❺ You don't open the door. ＿＿＿＿＿＿＿＿＿＿＿＿＿＿＿＿＿

2 「〜しましょう」という文を作りましょう。

❶ Sing songs. ＿＿＿＿＿＿＿＿＿＿＿＿＿＿＿＿＿

❷ Watch TV. ＿＿＿＿＿＿＿＿＿＿＿＿＿＿＿＿＿

❸ Eat lunch. ＿＿＿＿＿＿＿＿＿＿＿＿＿＿＿＿＿

❹ Play catch. ＿＿＿＿＿＿＿＿＿＿＿＿＿＿＿＿＿

3 *Write about yourself.*
命令文を使って、先生に3つ命令してみましょう。（ていねいに言いたい人は please を付けましょう。）

❶ ＿＿＿＿＿＿＿＿＿＿＿＿＿＿＿＿＿＿＿＿＿＿＿＿＿＿＿＿＿＿＿

❷ ＿＿＿＿＿＿＿＿＿＿＿＿＿＿＿＿＿＿＿＿＿＿＿＿＿＿＿＿＿＿＿

❸ ＿＿＿＿＿＿＿＿＿＿＿＿＿＿＿＿＿＿＿＿＿＿＿＿＿＿＿＿＿＿＿

CD 42

Do you have chocolate?

No, I don't.

Here it is. A valentine present from me!

Chant
CD 43/44

You have,

He has,

She has,

It has,

They all have it,

But I don't!

You have,

He has,

She has,

It has,

They all have it,

But I don't!

Excuse me...

I, You, We, They のときは have だけど、 **He, She, It** のときは has に変身します！

① 次の空欄をうめましょう。

	話す人	聞く人	話題になる人		
1人のとき	I		男の場合 ———	女の場合 ———	物の場合 ———
2人以上のとき			they		

② have または has を ═══ に入れて、文を完成しましょう。

❶ I ═══════════ a book.　❷ My brother ═══════════ many CDs.

❸ You and I ═══════════ two lessons today.

❹ Our city ═══════════ some beautiful parks.

③ ( ) 内に意味を、 ═══ には三人称の s が付いた形を書きましょう。

❶ know (〜を知る) knows　❷ like ( ) ═══════

❸ play ( ) ═══════　❹ want ( ) ═══════

❺ go ( ) ═══════　❻ live ( ) ═══════

❼ study ( ) ═══════　❽ do ( ) ═══════

CD 45

 Do you have any aunts or uncles?

 Yes, I do. I have two aunts and one uncle.
Mom has two sisters and one brother,
but dad doesn't have any.

Chant
CD 46/47

Do you like me?	**No, we don't.**
Yes, you do.	No, we don't.
Yes, you do.	No, we don't.
Yes, you do.	All right we like you.
Does he like me?	**No, he doesn't.**
Yes, he does.	No, he doesn't.
Yes, he does.	No, he doesn't.
Yes, he does.	All right he likes you.
Does she like me?	**No, she doesn't.**
Yes, she does.	No, she doesn't.
Yes, she does.	No, she doesn't.
Yes, she does.	All right she likes you.

Grammar

質問する時と「〜でない」という時は、ぼくがお手伝いします。sは追い出しますのでご安心を！

does

Does he like s mice?

あなたはいりません！

He **doesn't** like s snakes.

あなたも、必要ありません。

1 次の文を「〜しない」という否定文にしましょう。

❶ He likes English.

❷ My mother goes to school.

❸ My sister and I play baseball after school.

2 次の文を疑問文にしましょう。

❶ Your grandmother lives in New York.

❷ Tom studies English at school.

❸ Your father and mother play tennis.

3 *Write about yourself.*
次の語を使って人物を1人紹介しましょう。

years old / live / have / like / want

This is _____

Where? When? How? いろいろな疑問詞

CD 48

Let's meet in front of the post office.

When?

At seven thirty in the morning.

OK.

CD 49/50

Where, where, where?

Where shall we go?

To the park. To the park. Let's go to the park.

When, when, when?

When shall we go?

On Sunday. On Sunday. Let's go on Sunday.

How, how, how?

How shall we go?

By bike. By bike. Let's go by bike.

SUN

Grammar

いろいろな疑問詞

What
Where
Who
When
Whose

ぼくもお手伝いします。

many? How much?

わからないことがあれば、
まず、ぼくたちで
始めてみてください。

① 下から当てはまる語句を選んで書き入れましょう。

❶ どこ? _____

❷ なに? _____

❸ いつ? _____

❹ だれ? _____

❺ どのように? _____

❻ なぜ? _____

❼ 何時? _____

❽ いくつ? _____
（数）

❾ いくら? _____
（金額）

❿ だれのもの? _____

⓫ どのくらいの期間? _____

How long?　What?　Who?　Where?　When?　What time?　How much?　Whose?　Why?　How?　How many?

② 下線に注意して A の疑問文を完成しましょう。

❶ A: _____ does your father usually get up?

B: He usually gets up <u>at seven thirty</u>.

❷ A: _____ are you doing?

B: I'm doing <u>my homework</u> with my friends.

❸ A: _____ is your birthday?

B: My birthday is <u>July 30th</u>.

❹ A: _____ camera is this?

B: It's <u>my father's</u>.

③ *Write about yourself.*
①番の ❶〜⓫ の語句を使って、お友達に質問しましょう。

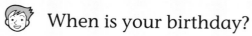
When is your birthday?

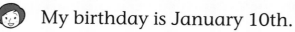
My birthday is January 10th.

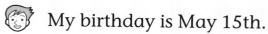
My birthday is May 15th.

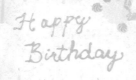

Chant
CD 52/53

Who has a birthday in January?

I have my birthday in January.

Lisa has her birthday in January.

Who has a birthday in May?

I have my birthday in May.

Larry has his birthday in May.

Grammar

1

次の質問文に対する答えを右から選び、線でむすびましょう。

❶ What time did you get up? •   • Ms. Baker does.

❷ Who teaches you English? •   • He is Mr. Yoshida.

❸ Who can answer this question? •   • At seven.

❹ Who is the leader? •   • Lisa can.

❺ Whose book is this? •   • It is my book.

❻ Who is that man? •   • Mr. Yoshida is.

2

Write about yourself.
あなた自身が考えて、次の質問に答えましょう。

❶ Who cooks dinner for you?

❷ Who cleans your room?

❸ Who can speak English?

❹ Which month comes after March?

❺ What day comes between Friday and Sunday?

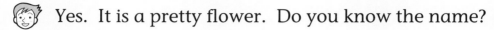

CD 54

Look at the flower. What a pretty flower!

Yes. It is a pretty flower. Do you know the name?

Yes. It is "dandelion".

Chant
CD 55/56

What a pretty, what a pretty, what a pretty girl I am!

What a noisy, what a noisy, what a noisy girl you are!

What a rude, what a rude, what a rude boy you are!

What a cool, what a cool, what a cool boy I am!

Grammar

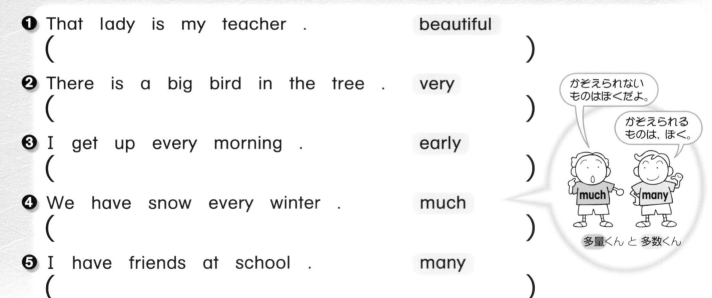

---

① ___ の語を入れるのに適切な位置に ∧ を書いて、英文の意味を書きましょう。

❶ That lady is my teacher .　　　**beautiful**
(　　　　　　　　　　　　　　　　　　　　)

❷ There is a big bird in the tree .　　**very**
(　　　　　　　　　　　　　　　　　　　　)

かぞえられない
ものはぼくだよ。

かぞえられる
ものは、ぼく。

❸ I get up every morning .　　　**early**
(　　　　　　　　　　　　　　　　　　　　)

❹ We have snow every winter .　　**much**
(　　　　　　　　　　　　　　　　　　　　)

much **many**

多量くん と 多数くん

❺ I have friends at school .　　　**many**
(　　　　　　　　　　　　　　　　　　　　)

---

② *Write about yourself.*
あなた自身のことについて、次の文を完成しましょう。

❶ My mother is very _____ .

❷ What a _____ friend I have!

❸ What a _____ teacher I have!

What a big lion!

a big lion

びっくりしたら
What がつくのか…

CD-57

 What were you doing when I called you last night? *

 I was cleaning my room.

Chant

CD-58/59

Busy, busy, busy.
We were busy all day long.

Mom was cooking all day long.
Dad was shopping all day long.
Rick was washing all day long.
I was cleaning all day long.
Ann was crying all day long.
Brownie was running all day long.

Busy, busy, busy.
We were busy all day long.

Grammar

Be(~です)ファミリーの
私たちは過去のことを言うとき、
変身します。

is **am** 変身！ **was**

are **were**

❶ 次の質問に答えて英文を完成しましょう。

❶ How is the weather today?

It is ＿＿＿＿＿＿＿＿＿＿＿＿＿ today.

❷ How was the weather yesterday?

It ＿＿＿＿＿＿＿ ＿＿＿＿＿＿＿＿＿＿ yesterday.

❷ 右の語群の中から正しい語を選んで書き入れましょう。

❶ You ＿＿＿＿＿＿＿＿ jogging in the park in the morning.

❷ Your cat ＿＿＿＿＿＿＿＿ sleeping on the roof last night.

❸ Our father ＿＿＿＿＿＿＿＿ working in his office now.

❹ I ＿＿＿＿＿＿＿ studying English last night.

❺ My brother and I ＿＿＿＿＿＿＿＿ watching TV last night.

❻ My teacher ＿＿＿＿＿＿＿＿ playing tennis then.

| is |
| am |
| are |
| were |
| was |

❸ Write about yourself.
自分のことについて書きましょう。

❶ What were you doing at seven o'clock this morning?

❷ What were you doing at eight o'clock last night?

❸ What was your mother doing at seven o'clock this morning?

20 I went to the market. 一般動詞の過去形 ①

Where did you go yesterday?

I went to a market with my mom.

Did you do your homework?

No. I didn't have any homework.

Chant

CD 61/62

Where did you go?	I went to the market.
What did you see?	I saw some fruit.
What did you buy?	I bought an apple.
How much did you pay?	I paid a dollar.
What did you do, then?	I ate the apple.

Not bad.

Grammar

過去のことを言うときは、動詞のうしろに **ed** がくっついてきます。

一緒にいようね！

play ed

もともと動詞の最後に **e** があるから **d** だけでいいよ。

like d

ぼくの場合は最後の字（**p**）がもう1ついるんだ。

stop p ed

私はちょっと変身してからです。

study → studi ed

ぼくたちは全く変身してしまうのです。

run ran   buy bought

みんな、ややこしいのね。私は変身しません。

cut

① 次の動詞の過去形を書いておぼえましょう。

❶ like _____   ❷ want _____   ❸ need _____

❹ stay _____   ❺ cut _____   ❻ clean _____

❼ have _____   ❽ take _____   ❾ study _____

❿ live _____   ⓫ see _____   ⓬ come _____

⓭ go _____   ⓮ make _____   ⓯ eat _____

② 次の（　）の中から適当な語を選びましょう。

❶ We (play / played) baseball yesterday.

❷ My sister (study / studies / studied) English last night.

❸ Ted (live / lives / lived) in Sapporo now.

❹ Yuka is a good girl. She (helps / helped) her mother every day.

❺ My father (buys / bought / buy) a present last Sunday.

❻ We (live / lived / lives) in Canada two years ago.

❼ I didn't (has / have / had) breakfast this morning.

CD 63

Mom, may I go out to play?

Did you do your homework?

Yes, I did. I did my homework. Look!

OK. You may go.

Chant

CD 64/65

Did you make your bed?
> Yes, I did. Yes, I did. I made my bed. Look!

Did you eat your lunch?
> Yes, I did. Yes, I did. I ate my lunch. Look!

Did you clean your room?
> Yes, I did. Yes, I did. I cleaned my room. Look!

Did you take a bath?
> Yes, I did. Yes, I did. I took a bath. Look!

Grammar

過去の「疑問文」や「否定文（〜しません）」になれば、ぼくがお手伝いします。

ひかえおろー！
これが目に入らぬか！
did でござるぞ。
元の形にもどれ!!

He **went** to school yesterday.

Did he **go** to school yesterday?
He **did** not **go** to school yesterday.
(didn't)

① 次の否定文を肯定文にしましょう。

❶ He didn't eat a hamburger yesterday.

❷ She didn't come to my house last Saturday.

❸ My father didn't buy a new computer for me.

② 次の文を疑問文にして、（　）内の語を使ってその質問に答えましょう。

❶ Lisa made some cookies. （ Yes ）

❷ She said good-bye to her friends. （ No ）

③ *Write about yourself.*
昨日したことを6つ書きましょう。

What did you do yesterday?

CD 66

 Let's go swimming. *

 I will make sandwiches and we will have a picnic on the beach.

 OK.

Chant

CD 67/68

It's a sunny day today. What will you do?

    I will go swimming.

    And I will eat lunch on the beach. × × ×

It's a rainy day today. What will you do?

    I will stay home.

    And I will read a book on the bed. × × ×

It's a snowy day today. What will you do?

    I will go outside.

    And I will take a walk in the park. × × ×

Grammar

1 次の下線の語句を（　　）内の語句に変えて、未来をあらわす文にしましょう。

❶ My uncle goes to Hawaii <u>every year</u>.（this summer）

❷ Where do you live <u>now</u>?（in future）

❸ What do you do <u>every Saturday</u>?（next Saturday）

❹ I am twelve years old <u>now</u>.（next year）

2 次の文を日本語にしましょう。

❶ I am going to stay home this afternoon.
（　　　　　　　　　　　　　　　　　　　　　　　　　　　）

❷ It's raining. We are not going to have a party in the garden.
（　　　　　　　　　　　　　　　　　　　　　　　　　　　）

3 次の日本語に合う英文を完成させましょう。

❶ 窓をあけてくれませんか？　（＿＿＿＿＿＿）you open the window?

❷ クッキーをいかがですか？　（＿＿＿＿＿＿）you have some cookies?

4 *Write about yourself.*
明日することを1つ書きましょう。

23 This is my bike. It's mine. 所有代名詞

CD 69

Is this my bike?

No, it isn't yours. It's Judie's.
Your bike is over there.

Thanks.

Chant CD 70/71

This is my bike.	It's mine. ××
This is your bike.	It's yours. ××
This is his bike.	It's his. ××
This is her bike.	It's hers. ××
This is their bike.	It's theirs. ××
This is our bike.	It's ours. ×!

Grammar

	私	あなた	彼	彼女	彼ら	私たち
～の	my	your	his	her	their	our
～のもの	mine	yours	his	hers	theirs	ours

「～の」なの？ それとも「～のもの」なの？ はっきりしてよ！

う～ん、わかんない…。

---

① 空欄に下の◯◯の中から適当な語を入れて、次の表を完成しましょう。

	私	あなた	彼	彼女	私たち	あなたたち	彼ら
～は							
～の							
～を～に							
～のもの							

my	me	mine	I	you	you	your	yours	his	his	him	he	her	her	she	hers
us	ours	we	our	them	they	theirs	their	yours	your	you	you				

---

② 次の（ ）の中から正しい語を選びましょう。

❶ (I / My / Me) am a student.

❷ Do you know (his / him) ?

❸ This bike is (you / your / yours) .

❹ This is (you / your / yours) bike.

❺ Does your father know (me / I / my) ?

❻ (She / Her / Hers) goes to junior high school.

---

③ *Write about yourself.*

例文を参考にして、友達の1人を紹介してみましょう。

例 This is my friend. His name is Larry. I like him very much.
He is kind and cheerful.

_____

_____

_____

_____

Hello. May I help you?

 Yes. I want a bag.

 How about this one?

 Do you have a bigger one?

 How about this one?

 OK. I'll take it.

This one is big, bigger than the other one.

This one is cheap, cheaper than the other one.

This one is nice, nicer than the other one.

    Big, bigger

    Cheap, cheaper

    Nice, nicer

I'll take the better one.

Grammar

「もっと〜です」というときは、
語尾に **er** をつけます。

「一番〜です」というときは、
語尾に **est** をつけます。

tall   taller   tallest

I am **tall**.

I am **taller**.
er

I am **the tallest!**
the
est

---

① 次の語の比較級と最上級を書きましょう。日本語を（　）の中に書きましょう。

比較級　　　　　　　　　　　最上級

❶ tall 　（　　　　　　）＿＿＿＿＿＿＿＿＿　＿＿＿＿＿＿＿＿＿

❷ cheap （　　　　　　）＿＿＿＿＿＿＿＿＿　＿＿＿＿＿＿＿＿＿

❸ nice 　（　　　　　　）＿＿＿＿＿＿＿＿＿　＿＿＿＿＿＿＿＿＿

❹ big 　（　　　　　　）＿＿＿＿＿＿＿＿＿　＿＿＿＿＿＿＿＿＿

❺ pretty （　　　　　　）＿＿＿＿＿＿＿＿＿　＿＿＿＿＿＿＿＿＿

❻ happy （　　　　　　）＿＿＿＿＿＿＿＿＿　＿＿＿＿＿＿＿＿＿

❼ hot 　（　　　　　　）＿＿＿＿＿＿＿＿＿　＿＿＿＿＿＿＿＿＿

※ 語尾の y を i に変えて er、est を付けたり、最後の文字を2つ重ねて er、est を付けることばもあるので注意しよう。

---

② （　）内の単語に er または est を付けて、次の文の（＝）に書き入れましょう。

❶ I am (＿＿＿＿＿＿＿＿＿) than my brother. 　　　　　　(young)

❷ This bag is (＿＿＿＿＿＿＿＿＿) than that one. 　　　　　(cheap)

❸ The moon is (＿＿＿＿＿＿＿＿＿) than the earth. 　　　　(small)

❹ Mt. Fuji is the (＿＿＿＿＿＿＿＿＿) mountain in Japan. 　(high)

❺ February is the (＿＿＿＿＿＿＿＿＿) of all the months in Japan. (cold)

---

③ *Write about yourself.*
次の空欄に好きな語句を入れて文をつくりましょう。

❶ I am ＿＿＿＿＿＿＿＿＿ than ＿＿＿＿＿＿＿＿＿ .

❷ ＿＿＿＿＿＿＿＿＿ is ＿＿＿＿＿＿＿＿＿ than ＿＿＿＿＿＿＿＿＿ .

❸ ＿＿＿＿＿＿＿＿＿ is the ＿＿＿＿＿＿＿ **est** in my class.

❹ ＿＿＿＿＿＿＿＿＿ is the ＿＿＿＿＿＿＿ **est** teacher in my school.

CD 75

How much does your dog weigh?

It weighs twenty-six kg.

Oh, he is just as heavy as my dog.

Chant

CD 76

My dog is as big as yours. ××

My dog is as big as you. ××

But I'm not as big as you. ×

You're bigger than I! ×

Grammar

ぼくたちと手をつなぐと「同じくらい」になるんだよ。

A is **as** big **as** B.

A は B と同じくらい大きい。

1 日本文に合うように適当な語句を入れて英文を完成しましょう。

❶ この家はあの家と同じくらい古い。

This house is ＿＿＿＿＿＿ old ＿＿＿＿＿＿ that house.

❷ この問題は私が思ったほどむずかしくない。

This problem is not ＿＿＿＿＿＿ difficult ＿＿＿＿＿＿ I thought.

2 次の英文を日本語にしましょう。

❶ Please speak more slowly. (＿＿＿＿＿＿＿＿＿＿＿＿＿＿)

❷ Please speak more loudly. (＿＿＿＿＿＿＿＿＿＿＿＿＿＿)

3 *Write about yourself.*
次の英文の中に適当な語句を入れて文を完成しましょう。

❶ ＿＿＿＿＿＿＿＿＿ is the busiest in my family.

❷ ＿＿＿＿＿＿＿＿＿ is the tallest in my class.

❸ I am much stronger than ＿＿＿＿＿＿＿＿＿ .

❹ I am the ＿＿＿＿＿＿＿＿＿ child in the world!?

❺ I am not as ＿＿＿＿＿＿＿＿＿ as my friend, ＿＿＿＿＿＿＿＿＿ .
(name)

❻ ＿＿＿＿＿＿＿＿＿ is the noisiest student in my class.

❼ ＿＿＿＿＿＿＿＿＿ is the most quiet student in my class.

4 *Write about yourself.*
あなたが思うことを書きましょう。

❶ Who is the most popular baseball player in Japan?
＿＿＿＿＿＿＿＿＿＿＿＿＿＿＿＿＿＿＿＿＿＿＿＿＿＿＿＿

❷ Which is more difficult, math or English?
＿＿＿＿＿＿＿＿＿＿＿＿＿＿＿＿＿＿＿＿＿＿＿＿＿＿＿＿

Lisa, why do we come to school every day?

Of course to study.
Why do you come to school?

Well... I come to school to meet friends.

CD 78/79

We go to the bakery	to buy some bread.
We go to the library	to read some books.
We go to the park	to ride a bike.
We go to school	to do WHAT?

Grammar

to＋動詞 で「〜するために」という目的をあらわします。

なぜ？ なぜ？

なんのためなのヨ！

Why?

What for?

そんなこといっても…
ただ「〜のために」だよ。

to

動詞

❶ 次の文の意味が通るように英文を完成しましょう。

❶ I went to the bookstore _____

❷ I have to study hard _____

❸ I bought some vegetables _____

❹ I went to the post office _____

> to make a salad ／ to mail the letters ／ to pass the exam ／ to buy some comic books

❷ 次の文の意味を書きましょう。

❶ I'm glad to get a present from him.
(   )

❷ I'm sorry to hear the news.
(   )

❸ I was surprised to see the movie star.
(   )

「〜して、〜」という意味もあります。

I am happy **to meet** you.
きみに会えてうれしい。

❸ *Write about yourself.*
次の文の意味が通るように英文を完成しましょう。

❶ I go to school to _____

❷ I want to go to _____ to _____

❸ I want to go to _____ to _____

27 I want something to eat. 不定詞の形容詞的用法

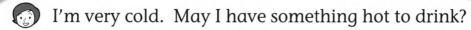

CD 80

I'm very cold. May I have something hot to drink?

How about a cup of hot chocolate?
I can make one for you.

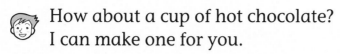

Chant

CD 81/82

I want something, something to eat.

    A hot dog, French fries, pizza and pie.

I want something, something to drink.

    Hot tea, iced tea, coffee and milk.

I want something, something to wear.

    A heavy coat, a warm sweater, mittens and socks.

I want something **to** + { drink. eat. wear. }

---

1 ( )内の語句をならべかえて日本文に合う英文をつくりましょう。

❶ なにか読むものを持っていますか？　Do you have (read / anything / to) ?

_____

❷ なにかあたたかい飲みものを買いましょう。　Let's buy (hot / something / drink / to).

_____

❸ あなたとお話しする時間はまったくありません。　I have (time / to / talk / with / no / you).

_____

---

2 === に適切な語を考えて、2語ずつ書きましょう。

❶ Something cold to drink

_____

❷ Something hot to drink

_____

❸ Something to eat

_____

❹ Something to read

_____

---

3 *Write about yourself.*
あなた自身のことについて考えて文を完成しましょう。

❶ I have no time to _____

❷ I need more time to _____

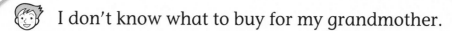

CD 83

I don't know what to buy for my grandmother.

Buy a necklace.

I don't know where to buy a necklace.

Go to the department store.

Do you know how to get to the department store?

Oh....

Chant

CD 84/85

Tell me, tell me everything.

I don't know what to do.

I don't know where to go.

I don't know when to go.

I don't know how to go.

I don't know anything.

No one knows what to do.

No one knows where to go.

No one knows when to go.

No one knows how to go.

No one knows anything.

Grammar

~ **how to do.**
どのようにするか

~ **where to do.**
どこでするか

~ **what to do.**
何をするか

~ **when to do.**
いつするか

I don't know…

---

1 次の（ ）内の語句を並べかえて日本文に合う英文をつくりましょう。

① 駅までの道を教えてください。
(Please / to / the station / show / how to get / me)

_____

_____

② 私はどちらを取っていいのかわかりません。
(which / take / don't / know / I / to)

_____

_____

③ どこに行けばいいか知っていますか？
(Do / where / you / to / know / go?)

_____

_____

④ 私は何を言えばいいのかわかりません。
(know / to / don't / what / I / say)

_____

_____

⑤ 私は次に何をするのかわかりませんでした。
(I / did / know / next / not / what / do / to)

_____

_____

---

2 *Write about yourself.*
あなた自身のことについて、次の質問に答えましょう。

① Do you know how to wear kimono?

_____

_____

② I want to buy a ticket for USJ. Do you know where to get it? ※USJ=Universal Studios Japan

_____

_____

③ Do you know where to go after this lesson?

_____

_____

86

What do you like to do when you are free? *

I like to watch a soccer game on TV.

Do you want to play soccer?

No, I don't. I just enjoy watching a game on TV.

Chant
CD 87/88

Listen to me. Listen to me.
I want you to study hard.

I'm listening. I'm listening.
I want you to leave me alone.

Listen to me. Listen to me.
I want you to clean your room.

I'm listening. I'm listening.
I want you to leave me alone.

Leave me alone. Leave me alone.

Listen to me. Listen to me….

Grammar

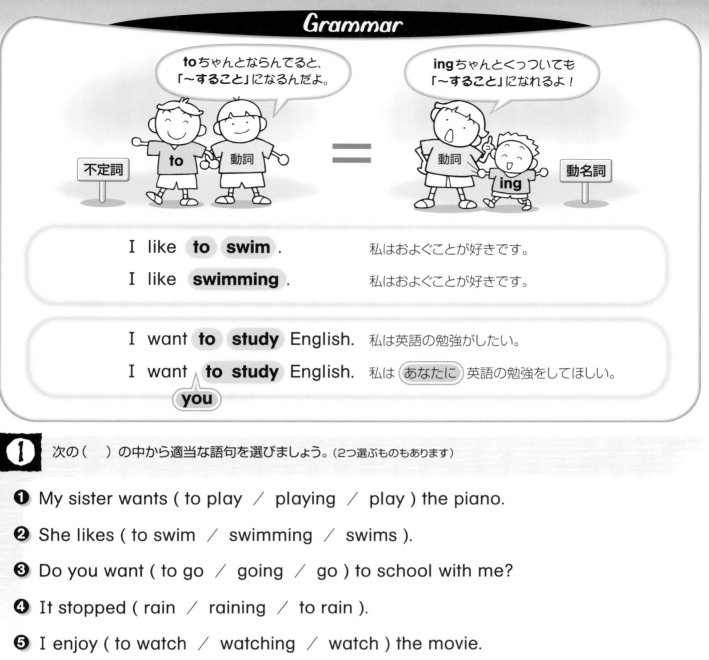

I like **to swim** . 　　私はおよぐことが好きです。

I like **swimming** . 　　私はおよぐことが好きです。

I want **to study** English. 　私は英語の勉強がしたい。

I want **to study** English. 　私は（あなたに）英語の勉強をしてほしい。
　　　you

---

❶ 次の（　）の中から適当な語句を選びましょう。（2つ選ぶものもあります）

❶ My sister wants (to play / playing / play) the piano.

❷ She likes (to swim / swimming / swims).

❸ Do you want (to go / going / go) to school with me?

❹ It stopped (rain / raining / to rain).

❺ I enjoy (to watch / watching / watch) the movie.

---

❷ *Write about yourself.*
　want to を使って、あなたが「したい」ことを3つ書きましょう。

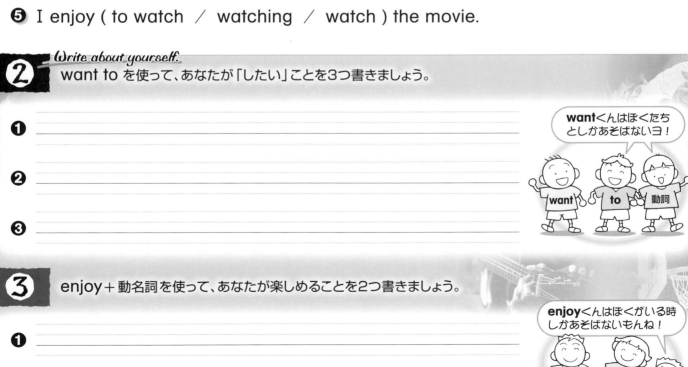

❶ _____

❷ _____

❸ _____

---

❸ enjoy＋動名詞を使って、あなたが楽しめることを2つ書きましょう。

❶ _____

❷ _____

The wine is made from grapes. 受け身

CD 89

Look! This wine is made by my father.

Really? Let me try.

No, no. You cannot drink.

Chant
CD 90

The wine is made, made from grapes.

The hill is covered, covered with vines.

The vine is full, full of grapes.

The grapes are cut, cut by a farmer.

The barrel is filled, filled with grapes.

The barrel is made, made of wood.

Everyone is pleased, pleased with the wine.

The wine is known, known to everyone.

Grammar

え!? まだふえるの？

ぼくも入れてー！

はじめまして！
過去分詞の spoken です。

speak 　 spoke 　 speaking 　 spoken

現在形 　 過去形 　 現在分詞

English is spoken by many people.

Be動詞 + 過去分詞 + by ... …に~される（されている）

※ byを使わないものもあります。

---

① 次の動詞の過去形、過去分詞形を調べて書きましょう。

	過去形	過去分詞形
❶ make （つくる）		
❷ cover （~で覆う）		
❸ know （知る）		
❹ use （使う）		
❺ see （見る）		
❻ speak （話す）		
❼ write （書く）		
❽ cut （切る）		

---

② 次の英文を日本語にしましょう。

❶ This watch is made in Japan.

(　　　　　　　　　　　　　　　　　　　　　　　　　　)

❷ Many good books are sold at this store.

(　　　　　　　　　　　　　　　　　　　　　　　　　　)

❸ This book is known to everyone.

(　　　　　　　　　　　　　　　　　　　　　　　　　　)

---

③ 次の文を、考えたり調べたりして完成しましょう。

❶ Tofu is made from _____

❷ Cheese is made from _____

This is the boy whom I love. 関係代名詞

Do you know the man who sings this song?

Yes. He is the one who wrote this song.

What is his name?

Oh, I forgot.

Chant

This is the boy whom I love.

This is the boy who loves me.

This is the house which I built.

This is the house where I live.

Well… life is not easy.

Grammar

きっちり説明したいときは、ぼくのあとに説明してください。

a flower

which

I saw on the mountain.

I bought for you.

is in the vase.

---

① 例にならって英文を整理して、全文の意味を書きましょう。

例 I have (a friend) who is from Italy.
(イタリア出身の友達)

「人」のことを説明するときは、ぼくを使ってください。

who

(意味) 私にはイタリア出身の友達がいます。)

❶ (The girl) who is playing the piano is my sister.
( )

(意味))

❷ Do you know (the man) who is standing over there?
( )

(意味))

❸ I have (a dog) which has short legs.
( )

(意味))

❹ This is (the house) which my father built.
( )

(意味))

❺ (The book) which I bought yesterday is very interesting.
( )

(意味))

---

② *Write about yourself.*
あなたが思うこととして、次の英文を完成しましょう。

❶ I have a friend who likes _____

❷ I know a man who can _____

❸ I have a teacher who _____

CD 93

Look at this picture. I drew a chicken.

A chicken doesn't have four legs!

You're right. A chicken has only two legs!

I've never seen a chicken with four legs.

Chant

CD 94/95

Have you ever seen a snake,
    a snake with legs?   NEVER.

Have you ever seen a pig,
    a pig with wings?   NEVER.

Have you ever seen a zebra,
    a zebra without stripes?   NEVER!

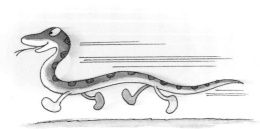

Grammar

have＋過去分詞 で「〜したことがある」という意味になります。

～したことがあるヨ!!

2人になると「**見たことがある**」になるんだ。

ぼくたちは3人で「**行ったことがある**」になるよ。

① 次の英文の意味を書きましょう。

❶ Have you been to Canada?

(　　　　　　　　　　　　　　　　　　　　　　　　　　)

❷ My father has been to London before.

(　　　　　　　　　　　　　　　　　　　　　　　　　　)

❸ I have read this book many times.

(　　　　　　　　　　　　　　　　　　　　　　　　　　)

❹ I have never heard such a beautiful song.

(　　　　　　　　　　　　　　　　　　　　　　　　　　)

② 次の動詞の過去形、過去分詞形を調べて書きましょう。

	過去形	過去分詞形
❶ read (読む)		
❷ hear (聞く)		
❸ eat (食べる)		
❹ catch (つかむ)		

③ *Write about yourself.*
あなた自身のことについて、次の質問に答えましょう。

❶ Have you ever seen a ghost?　　　　　　　　　　　　(ever＝今までに)

❷ Have you ever eaten a frog?

❸ Have you ever been to a foreign country?

❹ Have you ever seen a sumo wrestler before?

33 That makes him happy. いろいろな文型（五文型）

My dog can turn around.

My dog can turn the doorknob.
When I scold him, he sometimes turns pale.

You're kidding!

A dog is running. A dog is running.

That's my dog. ✕

I love my dog. I love my dog.

So I give him a bone. ✕

That makes him happy!

Grammar

文章をつなぐには、動詞の役目が大切です。動詞の種類によって、いろいろな文型があります。

ぼくたちは2人で文が作れるよ。

| I | go. |

私は　行く

私の仲間（**is, am, are, become, look**）は「〜は 〜です」という文を作ります。

私＝かわいい

| I | am | pretty. |

私は　です　かわいい

2人だけでは文ができないー！

はやく、はやくー！

| I | like | apples. |

私は　〜を好きです　りんご

ぼくは「人」に「物」を〜するという意味だから単語があと2つもくっついてくるんだ。

| I | give | him | a book. |

私は　人に物をあたえる　人　物

ぼくは「〜を〜にする」という意味であとに2つ単語がくっついてくるんだ。

| I | call | him | Tom. |

私は　〜を〜と呼ぶ　人　＝　名前

---

① 次の英文を日本語にしましょう。

❶ He runs very fast. (   )

❷ She is my teacher. (   )

❸ I wrote a long letter. (   )

❹ She showed me a picture. (   )

❺ That news made me sad. (   )

---

② Write about yourself.
次の英文の意味を確認しながら、文を完成させましょう。

❶ I live in _____
(意 味   )

❷ I am _____
(意 味   )

❸ I like _____
(意 味   )

❹ I will buy my mother _____ on her birthday.
(意 味   )

❺ If I have a dog, I will name it _____
(意 味 もしも犬を飼ったら、   )

CD 98

Let's go to the game center.

OK. But do you have any money?

No. Do you?

No, I don't.

Let's stay home, then.

Chant

CD 99

Let's go out if it is clear.

    Let's stay home if it is rainy.

Let's go out if you are free.

    Let's stay home if you are busy.

Let's go out if you've got some money.

    Let's go out if YOU've got some money.

OK. LET'S STAY HOME.

Grammar

ことばとことば、文と文をむすびつけるのが、ぼくたち接続詞の役目です。

接続詞 7 か国サミット会議

❶ 次の英文を日本語にしましょう。

❶ If you are in trouble, I will help you.
( )

❷ I am very tired because I went swimming in the morning.
( )

❸ I was very sleepy so I went to bed at eight o'clock.
( )

❹ Though it was raining, we played soccer.
( )

❺ I was watching TV when you called me last night.
( )

❻ You may go out after you finish your homework.
( )

❼ Come back home before it gets dark.
( )

❷ *Write about yourself.*
あなた自身のことについて、次の文を完成しましょう。

❶ If I am free tomorrow, I will _____.

❷ I usually _____ after I eat dinner.

❸ I usually _____ before I eat dinner.

❹ If I want to be in the top three in my class,

I will have to _____.

どれだけできたか確認しよう。
Achievement Target

先生は到達目標の数字をクラスのレベルに合わせて＿＿＿に書き入れてください。　Decide on the number of achievements according to the level of your students.

1 テキストのNo.1-12のチャンツのうち、＿＿＿個のチャンツを大きな声で暗誦できます。　No. ① ② ③ ④ ⑤ ⑥
Able to recite ＿＿＿ chants out of chants No. 1-12 in the textbook.　⑦ ⑧ ⑨ ⑩ ⑪ ⑫

2 先生が見せる12個の単語のうち、＿＿＿個の単語の複数形が言えます。
Able to say ＿＿＿ words in their plural form out of the twelve my teacher shows.

3 This is a …, That is a …, These are … …s, Those are … …s を使って教室内にあるものを英語で説明できます。
Able to describe objects in the classroom using "This is a …" "These are … …s" and "Those are … …s."

4 I have … in my bag. を使って自分のカバンに入っているものを＿＿＿個、英語で言えます。
Able to say ＿＿＿ things in my bag using "I have … in my bag."

5 今日の日にち、曜日、天気を英語で言うことができます。　Able to say today's date, the day and weather.

6 テキストのNo.13-25のチャンツのうち、＿＿＿個のチャンツを大きな声で暗誦できます。　No. ⑬ ⑭ ⑮ ⑯ ⑰ ⑱
Able to recite ＿＿＿ chants out of chants No. 13-25 in the textbook.　⑲ ⑳ ㉑ ㉒ ㉓ ㉔ ㉕

7 命令形〔否定命令形〕を使って先生に＿＿＿個命令することができます。（Pleaseをつけて）
Able to give ＿＿＿ commands to my teacher using the imperative form and 'Please'.

8 友達を1人選び、その友達を＿＿＿個以上の文章を使ってみんなに紹介することができます。
Able to introduce a friend with more than ＿＿＿ sentences.

9 形容詞を使って＿＿＿個、文章が言えます。　Able to make ＿＿＿ sentences using adjectives.

10 昨夜の午後9時に何をしていたかを英語で言えます。　Able to say what I did last night at nine o'clock.

11 先生が見せる15の動詞のうち、12の過去形が言えます。
Able to say twelve verbs in their past tense out of the fifteen my teacher shows.

12 昨日したことを＿＿＿個言えます。　Able to say ＿＿＿ things I did yesterday.

13 明日することを＿＿＿個言えます。　Able to say ＿＿＿ things I am going to do tomorrow.

14 my, his, her, our を使って、自分の名前、友達の名前と、自分達の先生の名前を言えます。
Able to say my name, my friend's name and our teacher's name using 'my', 'his', 'her' and 'our'.

15 身近なものを taller, bigger, older, younger, more famous, more popular, more expensive の中の語彙を
使って＿＿＿個英文にできます。　Able to make ＿＿＿ sentences about daily objects using 'taller', 'bigger', 'older',
'younger', 'more famous', 'more popular' and 'more expensive'.

16 テキストのNo.26-34のチャンツのうち、＿＿＿個のチャンツを大きな声で暗誦できます。　No. ㉖ ㉗ ㉘ ㉙ ㉚
Able to recite ＿＿＿ chants out of chants No. 26-34 in the textbook.　㉛ ㉜ ㉝ ㉞

17 enjoy を使って、自分が楽しめることを＿＿＿個言えます。　Able to say ＿＿＿ things I like to do using 'enjoy'.

18 先生が見せる15の動詞のうち、12の過去分詞形を言うことができます。
Able to say twelve verbs in their past participle out of the fifteen my teacher shows.

19 I know a man who can …. を使って、自分の知っている人を紹介できます。
Able to introduce someone I know using "I know a man who can …"

20 If I have a hundred thousand yen, I will buy …. を使って、自分が買うであろう物を英語で言うことができます。
Able to say things I would buy using "If I have a hundred thousand yen, I will buy …"

Certificate of Achievement

CHANTS for Grammar

Awarded to _____

this _____ day of _____,

for your great effort in

CHANTS for Grammar

Signed _____